"*Pure Joy* sho[ws] [how the] joy of the L[ord...] lives are either overwhelmed or transformed for good by our choices in difficult moments. Lorna chose to praise God in the very first moments she received news of her husband's suicide and walked in a supernatural joy that the Bible teaches is ours. May you be motivated to know the same joy in your life!"

—James and Catherine Randall, Pastors
City Centre Church
Saskatoon, Saskatchewan

"*Pure Joy* is a powerful reinforcement that instills within us as Believers an understanding that joy is a spiritual force that empowers us to go through tests, trials, and tribulations with joy and a peace that passes all understanding."

—Dez and Joy Desnomie, Pastors
David's Heart Ministries
Saskatoon, Saskatchewan

"Reading this book is a must for every Believer. I highly recommend it. You will learn to walk in joy in every situation you encounter in your life as you put into practice the seven steps outlined in this book. You will realize that only by having an intimate relationship with Jesus could the author live in pure joy. I was encouraged, and you will be too, at how trusting in the Lord and the joy of the Lord has carried Lorna through trials that would leave many Christians wounded and defeated. I have known Lorna for many years and she has truly lived what she writes."

—Pat Frost, Teacher
Lifeway Christian Academy
Saskatoon, Saskatchewan

"Very impacting, life changing, I couldn't put it down! This is truly a testimony to the power joy has in our life when we choose to embrace it."

—Carol Whyte, Teacher
Bengough, Saskatchewan

Making the Choice to Rejoice

PURE
Joy

LORNA HANISHEWSKI

PURE JOY
Copyright © 2019 by Lorna Hanishewski

All rights reserved. Neither this publication nor any part of this publication may be reproduced or transmitted in any form or by any means, electronic or mechanical, including photocopying, recording or any information storage and retrieval system, without permission in writing from the author.

The content of this publication is based on actual events. Names may have been changed to protect individual privacy.

Unless otherwise indicated, all scripture quotations are taken from the Holy Bible, NEW INTERNATIONAL VERSION®, NIV® Copyright © 1973, 1978, 1984, 2011 by Biblica, Inc.® Used by permission. All rights reserved worldwide. Scripture quotations marked (AMP) are taken from the Amplified® Bible, Copyright © 1954, 1958, 1962, 1964, 1965, 1987 by The Lockman Foundation. Used by permission. Scripture quotations marked (GNT) are taken from the Good News Translation® (Today's English Version, Second Edition), Copyright © 1992 American Bible Society. All rights reserved. Bible text from the Good News Translation (GNT) is not to be reproduced in copies or otherwise by any means except as permitted in writing by American Bible Society, 1865 Broadway, New York, NY 10023. Scripture quotations marked (GW) are taken from GOD'S WORD®, © 1995 God's Word to the Nations. Used by permission of Baker Publishing Group. Scripture quotations marked (ESV) are taken from The Holy Bible, English Standard Version® (ESV®), copyright © 2001 by Crossway, a publishing ministry of Good News Publishers. Used by permission. All rights reserved. Scripture quotations marked (TPT) are taken from The Passion Translation®. Copyright © 2017, 2018 by Passion & Fire Ministries, Inc. Used by permission. All rights reserved. ThePassionTranslation.com. Scripture quotations marked (MSG) are taken from The Message. Copyright © 1993, 1994, 1995, 1996, 2000, 2001, 2002. Used by permission of NavPress Publishing Group. Scripture quotations marked (NASB) are taken from the New American Standard Bible®, Copyright © 1960, 1962, 1963, 1968, 1971, 1972, 1973, 1975, 1977, 1995 by The Lockman Foundation. Used by permission. Scripture quotations marked (KJV) are taken from the Holy Bible, King James Version, which is in the public domain. Scripture quotations marked (NKJV) are taken from the New King James Version®. Copyright © 1982 by Thomas Nelson, Inc. Used by permission. All rights reserved. Scripture quotations marked (AMPC) are taken from the Amplified® Bible (AMPC), Copyright © 1954, 1958, 1962, 1964, 1965, 1987 by The Lockman Foundation. Used by permission. www.Lockman.org. Scripture quotations marked (CEV) are taken from the Contemporary English Version Copyright © 1991, 1992, 1995 by American Bible Society, Used by Permission. Scripture quotations marked (FBV) are taken from the Free Bible Version Copyright © 2018 Dr. Jonathan Gallagher. Scripture quotations marked (NLT) are taken from the Holy Bible, New Living Translation, copyright ©1996, 2004, 2007 by Tyndale House Foundation. Used by permission of Tyndale House Publishers, Inc., Carol Stream, Illinois 60188. All rights reserved. Scripture quotations marked (NCV) are taken from the New Century Version®. Copyright © 2005 by Thomas Nelson. Used by permission. All rights reserved. Scripture quotations marked (CSB) are taken from The Christian Standard Bible. Copyright © 2017 by Holman Bible Publishers. Used by permission. Christian Standard Bible®, and CSB® are federally registered trademarks of Holman Bible Publishers, all rights reserved.

ISBN: 978-1-4866-1779-1 Printed in Canada

Word Alive Press
119 De Baets Street, Winnipeg, MB R2J 3R9
www.wordalivepress.ca

WORD ALIVE PRESS

MIX
Paper from responsible sources
FSC® C103567

Cataloguing in Publication may be obtained through Library and Archives Canada

I would like to dedicate this book in loving memory of my husband, Clarence John Hanishewski (February 23, 1963–April 23, 2014).

> *With a loud command and with the shout of the chief angel and a blast of God's trumpet, the Lord will return from heaven. Then those who had faith in Christ before they died will be raised to life. Next, all of us who are still alive will be taken up in the clouds together with them to meet the Lord in the sky. From that time on we will all be with the Lord forever.*
> —1 Thessalonians 4:16–17, CEV

CONTENTS

	Acknowledgements	ix
	Introduction	xi
1.	Pure Joy	1
2.	Choose Joy!	16
3.	What Is Real Joy?	30
4.	Fullness of Joy	36
5.	Keys to Joy—Part One	44
6.	Keys to Joy—Part Two	61
	Conclusion	81

ACKNOWLEDGEMENTS

I would like to acknowledge and thank my friend and sister in the Lord, Pastor Catherine Randall, for her continual encouragement in my writing of this book. Her countless hours assisting me in the proofreading and editing, and in checking the accuracy of scripture and readability of the manuscript, have been invaluable. You are a blessing from the Lord.

I would also like to acknowledge and thank my friends and intercessors Catherine Randall, Pat Frost, Debbie Lee, and Annette Koss for their ongoing support, encouragement, and prayers for me during the writing of this book.

INTRODUCTION

Joy is an essential element in every believer's life. It's invaluable—a treasure to be discovered within our recreated spirit. When joy is uncovered, our lives become an oasis, a place of great contentment. Joy is watered by faith, enriched by our thankfulness, and bolstered through our praise and prayers. Joy becomes a fountain that floods our lives with uncontainable joy!

Many people don't understand the importance of joy in their lives. To live this Christian life as overcomers, we need the spirit of joy operating in our lives daily. Only by spending time in the presence of the Lord, obeying His Word, and following His command to rejoice will we grow in our understanding of joy.

Joy is a fruit of the Spirit that resides inside every born again child of God by the Holy Spirit. A joyless Christian hasn't learned to give God first place in their life. When you surrender your life to the control of the Holy Spirit, you become a joyful person. We must live by faith, believing that God's goodness is with us despite the circumstances. When we trust the Lord and obey His commands, we have a most enjoyable life.

When we learn to live joyfully, we become thankful, prayerful, and a student of the Word of God. We enjoy serving and sharing our faith in Christ. The joy of the Lord will be our strength. As we abide in Him, we experience pure joy—which is beyond description. The fruit of the Spirit will come to maturity in our lives and be manifest for everyone to see. Many will be drawn to God because of the fruits of love, joy, peace, kindness, patience, gentleness, faith, goodness, and self-control we display.

I have written this book out of my desire to see God's people walking in the fullness of joy and to encourage them with the revelation I've been given on this topic. I've experienced much joy over the years as I've endeavoured to develop a close, intimate relationship with the Lord; however, I know that I have only come to experience and understand the surface of the joy-filled life, and I want to continue to seek the Lord for greater revelation.

PURE JOY
Chapter One

"... consider it pure joy ... whenever you face trials of many kinds."

—James 1:2

Joy is a by-product of our relationship with the Holy Spirit that we can access at any time, even in tragedy and great difficulty. It might sound absurd to have joy when it doesn't seem very natural in the moment. How could we rejoice or choose to be joyful in the midst of tragedy or trying circumstances? The answer to that question lies in our understanding of joy, what it is and isn't, where it originates from, and how we can access it in our lives.

What does it mean to count it all joy? When facing troubling circumstances, we can choose right at that moment to learn from the situation and believe that the joy of the Lord is our strength, enabling us to press through difficulty: "*Be assured that the testing of your faith [through experience] produces endurance [leading to spiritual maturity, and inner peace]*" (James 1:3, AMP).

We can count it all joy in the midst of the most horrific situations, because the Joy Giver is with us in the middle of it all. We can look past the immediate pain to the future.

The trials and afflictions we face here on earth, no matter how difficult, are only temporary. As believers in Christ, our faith assures us of an eternal future with the Lord: "*You love him, although you have not seen him, and you believe in him, although you do not now see him. So you rejoice with a great and glorious joy which words cannot express*" (1 Peter 1:8, GNT).

There's no greater example for us to follow than Jesus Himself. He anticipated the future joy He'd experience when people accept His free gift of salvation. This didn't lessen the pain of the cross, but it enabled Him to endure it: "... *He saw the joy ahead of him, so he endured death on the cross and ignored the disgrace it brought him* ..." (Hebrews 12:2, GW).

Other than Jesus, no one in the New Testament went through more trials than the apostle Paul, yet he spoke of finding joy in those troubling times: "*Always, be joyful. Never stop praying. Whatever happens, give thanks because it is God's will in Christ Jesus that you do this*" (1 Thessalonians 5:16–18, GW); "*Rejoice in the Lord always; again I will say, rejoice!*" (Philippians 4:4, ESV). Paul demonstrated this joy when he and Silas were in prison.

Paul had cast out a spirit of divination from a slave girl. This infuriated her owners, as they made lots of money from her fortune telling. Paul and Silas were beaten, put in stocks, and placed in the dungeon of the jail. They chose to rejoice in the midnight hour, causing the Lord to send an earthquake that broke apart the prison, setting them and every other prisoner free. Their decision to make the best of a horrible situation enabled God to move on their behalf. By choosing to rejoice instead of grumbling, complaining, or feeling sorry for themselves, Paul and Silas counted it all joy. In bad situations, we can do the same and prevent the circumstances from shipwrecking our lives. Life won't always be smooth sailing, but we can be content and joyful in all situations. We can completely trust in the Word of God, because every word is full of truth:

"*Every promise from the faithful God is pure and proves to be true*" (Proverbs 30:5a, TPT).

Paul trusted God. He knew that no matter what happened, God would take care of Him, so he was content with his life and full of joy.

I've worked much harder, been jailed more often, beaten up more times than I can count, and at death's door time after time. I've been flogged five times with the Jews' thirty-nine lashes, beaten by Roman rods three times, pummeled with rocks once. I've been shipwrecked three times, and immersed in the open sea for a night and a day. In hard traveling year in and year out, I've had to ford rivers, fend off robbers, struggle with friends, struggle with foes. I've been at risk in the city, at risk in the country, endangered by desert sun and sea storm, and betrayed by those I thought were my brothers. I've known drudgery and hard labor, many a long and lonely night without sleep, many a missed meal, blasted by the cold, naked to the weather. And that's not the half of it, when you throw in the daily pressures and anxieties of all the churches.

—2 Corinthians 11:23–28, MSG

After going through these struggles, Paul twice tells the church at Philippi to rejoice as he writes to them from a Roman prison. We experience true joy when we trust in the Lord in every situation.

In Acts 5, the apostles are beaten and told not to speak in the name of Jesus. Upon being released, they go away rejoicing!

> *So they departed from the presence of the council, rejoicing that they were counted worthy to suffer shame for His name. And daily in the temple, and in every house, they did not cease teaching and preaching Jesus as the Christ.*
>
> —Acts 5:41–42, NASB

Most of us know someone who's had to face a difficult circumstance, such as a terminal illness, a life-threatening situation, or the loss of someone close to them, but never lost their joy. They stayed upbeat, positive, and faithful to the end. People can maintain their trust in God through trials because they have the assurance that God is always with them. If they lose the battle for life, they ultimately win the victory over death because of their faith and acceptance of God's eternal life through Jesus Christ. We can rejoice no matter what is going on, because our names are written in the Lamb's Book of Life, and our lives are hidden in Christ.

Joy is never subject to circumstances. Several years ago, my husband, Clarence, received a quarter section of farmland from his mom. The rest of the land was to go to his younger brother. For whatever reason, his brother felt that all the land should go to him, so he became angry and jealous of Clarence. One summer day, Clarence asked Graham, a friend who farmed nearby, if he'd bale the hay for him. His brother found out that Graham was in the field and became very upset. He drove his car onto the field and began shooting at him. Graham was injured but managed to call his wife and the police. The police, the ambulance, and his wife all showed up at the scene. The first thing Graham's wife said to the police was, "You have to warn Clarence and Lorna. I know he's going to go after them."

A few minutes after the shooting, we received two warning phone calls. The first was from Clarence's oldest sister, who said that their brother had shot Graham, come back to the house, grabbed some bullets, and said, "I'm going to get Clarence." The second was from the RCMP telling us what had happened and that Graham's wife, Marcia, believed he was going to come after us.

The police asked us who lived at our acreage. At the time it was just my son, my husband, and myself. We were also taking care of a friend's young boy for a few days. The police told us to leave the premises as soon as possible, so we gathered up some clothes and a few necessities, and left. We knew it would take Clarence's brother at least three hours to get to our place from the farm.

We immediately began to pray for Graham, Clarence's brother, and our own protection. As soon as we did, great peace and joy began to manifest. We experienced a great calm and a sense that God was in control. This brought us great joy.

Pure Joy

We stayed at a friend's home that night. Even though we'd prayed, the enemy didn't give up easily, and it was a very stressful situation. My husband was understandably concerned about his friend and upset with his brother. The police kept calling to ask him questions and let him know what they were doing at the acreage. They staked out the house and hid in the trees, waiting for his brother to show up.

Clarence had a hard time falling asleep that night because of the turmoil he was dealing with. His brother took longer to get to the acreage than we expected, and the police questioned whether or not he would show up. Clarence told them, "Don't leave; he will come." We prayed that the police would stay put until he showed up.

I remember saying to Clarence: "You need to forgive your brother right now and pray protection upon him and the police, and also that he will give himself up without a struggle." We prayed, and I began to smile as God's presence overwhelmed us.

"How can you smile and be happy at a time like this?" Clarence asked. "It's not funny; it's serious."

"I know," I replied, "but God is so good, and we're all safe. We just need to put our trust in Him."

He said "okay" and turned over and went to sleep.

Early the next morning, Clarence got a phone call from the police saying that his brother had shown up at the acreage, and they had arrested him. They said that he'd gotten out of his car, headed to the trunk, and was about to open it when they put the floodlights on him. He'd given himself up right away. He had rifles and a shotgun in the trunk of the car.

I learned from that situation that when you choose to pray to God and trust Him, He will protect you and those you love. When you remain calm instead of panicking or becoming fearful, and allow His presence to overtake you, you will experience joy and peace in the Holy Spirit. Joy comes from His presence and gives us the strength to handle fear and stress in any situation, no matter how threatening.

It can be easier to let joy arise in us when facing a very difficult situation as opposed to a relatively minor trial. In fiery trials, we quickly realize that we have no other option for accessing joy within us. We can draw from Jesus, the true vine, because we're connected as branches, and joy is a fruit that grows in us. Letting little troubles bother us causes us to quench the fruit of the Spirit and prevents joy from manifesting in our lives. In the seemingly small circumstances of life, we don't run to the Lord first but instead try to handle them on our own. We often find ourselves complaining, causing us to lose our joy. We decide to go it alone and quickly become discouraged and downcast.

> *You must catch the troubling foxes, those sly little foxes that hinder our relationship. For they raid our budding vineyard of love to ruin what I've planted within you. Will you catch them and remove them for me? We will do it together.*
> —Song of Solomon 2:15, TPT

Pure Joy

Through adversity, we learn to grow and discover that much good can come to our lives. Jesus Christ gives us the ability to rejoice our way through anything. We become more resilient to life's circumstances when we learn to rejoice. When we participate in joyful praise to the Lord, we fix our attention on Him instead of our problems. We're better able to see the good that can come from every negative situation when we rejoice wholeheartedly with thanksgiving. It changes the atmosphere around us and in our hearts. When we count it all joy, choosing to let it rise up in us by the Holy Spirit, we gain the strength to endure hardships. God imparts great joy to us in those moments.

All of us go through trials; no one is exempt, but overcoming trials with joy can become a part of our testimony. We've all said or heard it said, "But you don't understand what I've been through." The Bible tells us that we can overcome: "*And they overcame him by the blood of the Lamb, and by the word of their testimony ...*" (Revelation 12:11a, KJV).

I went through a difficult season of trying circumstances. It seemed like I faced one thing after another. Yet it was also a time of great joy and spiritual growth in my life. The most difficult storm took place a few years ago when I received some shocking news. I was in Kenya on a mission trip when I received a phone call telling me that my husband had passed away. Tragically, he had died by his own hand. Hearing something like that is paralyzing—your mind and body go into a state of shock, so you can't think right. Joy is definitely not the first reaction!

At first it doesn't seem real, but then a multitude of emotions erupt—everything from anger to overwhelming fear.

As I began to process what had happened, in the middle of the night in a remote village in Kenya, I heard that still, small voice say to me, "Praise Me!" As my friend and I obeyed the Holy Spirit and began to praise the Lord, joy bubbled up, even in the middle of the great sorrow I was feeling. Praise lifts us up and brings supernatural joy as it transports us into the very presence of the Lord. At that time, I was faced with the choice to either go with my emotions or to praise God. I chose to obey the Holy Spirit and praise the Lord. That decision radically changed my life and helped me overcome sorrow and grief. I took my focus off myself and put it on the Lord. I clung to the truth that my God is good despite the difficulties I face. My thinking shifted, and I experienced overcoming joy. Even my husband's death couldn't take it from me. It's amazing to experience a grace and strength that only comes from God. The Word of God became more than just words on a page ... it was my strength and saving grace: "*Do not sorrow, for the joy of the Lord is your strength*" (Nehemiah 8:10b, NKJV); "*... in Your presence is fullness of joy...*" (Psalm 16:11b, NKJV).

Grieving is a healthy response to the death of a loved one, but our belief in the truth of Jesus's death, burial, and resurrection brings comfort and joy. We know that our separation is only temporary and that we have all of eternity to spend with the ones we love. They have gone to their eternal home ahead of us, but we will join them one day.

Pure Joy

I found comfort in the knowledge that my husband had received Jesus as his Saviour many years before his death. When he passed from this life, I know he went to heaven. He had lost hope but not his salvation. It brought me great peace and joy to know the truth of this as expressed in this Bible passage: "*We live with a joyful confidence, yet at the same time we take delight in the thought of leaving our bodies behind to be at home with the Lord*" (2 Corinthians 5:8, TPT).

We all experience times of sadness and grief, but we must choose not to live there. When we meditate on the Word of God, we discover that we can draw on joy within our recreated spirit when we need it: "*So keep your thoughts continually fixed on all that is authentic and real, honorable and admirable, beautiful and respectful, pure and holy, merciful and kind. And fasten your thoughts on every glorious work of God, praising him always*" (Philippians 4:8, TPT).

Joy isn't an option. We are commanded in scripture to rejoice. Here are three definitions of the word "command' taken from different sources:

- Collins English Dictionary: "If someone in authority commands you to do something, they tell you that you must do it."[1]

---

[1] *Collins*, s.v. "command," accessed November 18, 2018, https://www.collinsdictionary.com/dictionary/english/command.

- Merriam-Webster: "implies the power to make arbitrary decisions and compel obedience."[2]
- Dictionary.com: "any order given by one in authority."[3]

Paul commanded the Philippians and the Thessalonians to rejoice: "*Rejoice always*" (1 Thessalonians 5:16).

Rejoicing is not an option or a suggestion—it's a command. When we obey God in this, He overwhelms us with His joy. We have an obligation as Christians to be joyful. Being joyful is a matter of our will. We can rejoice even when we don't have any desire to. Being thankful is the key to walking in joy. Rejoicing and thanksgiving go hand in hand in our lives. Paul continues in 1 Thessalonians 5:18 by writing that it's God's will for us who are in Christ Jesus to be thankful in everything. It's in Christ we rejoice and are thankful, not in the circumstances.

"*I can do all things through Christ who strengthens me*" (Philippians 4:13, NKJV). Paul could do anything because he was strengthened through rejoicing in the Lord always. Rejoicing is an attitude—we choose to think and act as God commands us to, no matter the storm.

---

[2] *Merriam-Webster*, s.v. "command," accessed November 18, 2018, https://www.merriam-webster.com/dictionary/command.

[3] *Dictionary.com*, s.v. "command," accessed November 9, 2018, https://www.dictionary.com/browse/command?s=ts.

Pure Joy

Rejoicing is a powerful weapon in a believer's arsenal. It helps us think clearly by fixing our minds on Christ instead of problems, and it gives us the strength to endure hardships. We are set free! When our heart is set on rejoicing, adversity can't keep us down. Joy will always cause us to rise above difficulties.

It takes faith to count it all joy. Joy is a spiritual discipline. We choose to be joyful because we walk by faith and not by what we see. We make a choice to put on the garment of praise no matter the difficulties. It would have been easy for Paul and Silas to give way to their feelings and become heavy-hearted and depressed, especially knowing they were wrongly accused, beaten, and imprisoned. Their choice to put on praise was remarkable. It brought them freedom, spiritually and physically, from imprisonment: "... *The garment of praise for the spirit of heaviness ...*" (Isaiah 61:3b, NKJV).

Jesus is the source of all godly joy, so true joy can only be found in our connection to Him. God wants us to have joy to the fullest measure, and it's only in His presence that we experience fullness of joy. Paul and Silas experienced and displayed abundant joy that night in prison. Their trust was in God, and the Lord vindicated them by setting them free. What a testimony!

"*But let all those rejoice who put their trust in You; Let them ever shout for joy, because You defend them; Let those also who love Your name be joyful in You*" (Psalm 5:11, NKJV). God wants us to share the gift of joy with others. Joy came to us from the Father in the form of His Son and is manifested in our lives through the Holy Spirit. When Jesus was born, an angel appeared to the shepherds, bringing them the good news:

Pure Joy

But the angel said to them, Do not be afraid; for behold, I bring you good news of a great joy which will come to all the people. For to you is born this day in the town of David a Savior, Who is Christ (the Messiah) the Lord!

—Luke 2:10–11, AMPC

Sharing the good news of Jesus with others brings us joy. The apostles were beaten for preaching and teaching in the name of Jesus, but after their release, they continued to rejoice and preach and teach in Jesus' name. They considered it pure joy that they were found worthy to suffer shame for His name.

Jesus Christ was full of joy, but He was also "... *a Man of sorrows ... acquainted with grief* ..." (Isaiah 53:3b, NKJV). The writer of the book of Hebrews echoes the Psalms when he writes: "... *Therefore God, Your God, has anointed You with the oil of gladness more than Your companions*" (Hebrews 1:9b, NKJV). As a man, Jesus identified with our sorrows and griefs, but He was also anointed with the oil of gladness. Jesus promised joy to His disciples, and I believe that extends to all of us who are disciples of the Lord today: "*These things I have spoken to you, that My joy may remain in you, and that your joy may be full*" (John 15:11, NKJV).

Several years ago, a tragic accident took place in our home when a young teen took a 22-caliber shotgun and pointed it at a young man and pulled the trigger. He was just goofing around, but he was totally unaware that a bullet had been left in the gun. The young man was killed instantly. A large number of church friends and family were at our house that evening celebrating our daughter's birthday and going away party, as she was leaving to spend several months with her sister in Indonesia. What stands out most in my memory from that day was the overwhelming peace that came over us all. Instead of chaos, there was calm. We began to pray and continued praying that evening at our church together. That night I went to the child care centre I directed and slept for a few short hours on the couch. When I was finally alone and able to reflect on what had happened, I didn't react with fear or anger but peace and joy. As I lay on that couch praying and rejoicing, the words "all is well" kept running through my head. His presence always brings joy, even in the midst of great tragedy and sadness.

Just like Christ, we can be acquainted with grief and godly sorrow and be anointed with the oil of gladness simultaneously. We can consider it all joy when we experience grief, sorrows, trials, and afflictions and be blessed with the oil of gladness as we rejoice in the midst of it all. The Word of God tells us that nothing can separate us from the love of God. It's the same with joy—nothing, no person or circumstance, can prevent us from abiding in the joy of the Lord. God commands us in His Word to rejoice continually. It's a matter of obedience! We must choose to rise above all the troubles we face and by faith access the joy that comes from the Holy Spirit.

Now may God, the inspiration and fountain of hope, fill you to overflowing with uncontainable joy and perfect peace as you trust in him. And may the power of the Holy Spirit continually surround your life with his super-abundance until you radiate with hope!

—Romans 15:13, TPT

Just like God's love, godly joy comes from the Spirit of the Lord. We can experience pure, overflowing joy anywhere, anytime, no matter what we're facing. We have a choice to allow joy to spring forth from us by Christ's Spirit that dwells within each of us. It's not dependent on circumstances but on relationship. If we're living a presence-based life in which the Holy Spirit is the dominating influence for everything we say and do, then joy should reign continuously in our hearts and lives no matter what's happening around us. We should be able to say, "*This is the day the Lord has made; We will rejoice and be glad in it*" (Psalm 118:24, NKJV).

CHOOSE JOY!
Chapter Two

"I will sing with joy because of you; I will sing praise to you, Almighty God."

—Psalm 9:2, GNT

Everything we do in life is a choice, whether something simple like what to eat for breakfast or as important as the person we marry. The decisions we make, big or small, affect our lives either positively or negatively. Our choices always carry consequences.

But if you don't want to worship the Lord, then choose right now! Will you worship the same idols your ancestors did? Or since you're living on land that once belonged to the Amorites, maybe you'll worship their gods. I won't. My family and I are going to worship and obey the Lord!

—Joshua 24:15, CEV

God gave us a free will, but what does that mean? The Merriam Webster dictionary defines it simply as a "voluntary choice or decision."[4] The Bible reveals God's will for mankind when we choose to obey or disobey His will. It's always our choice whether or not to obey. The Bible is full of commands, but we must choose to follow them.

From the very beginning of humanity's existence, God gave us instructions. He gave Adam the very first command in Genesis:

And the Lord God commanded the man, saying, "You may freely (unconditionally) eat [the fruit] from every tree of the garden; but [only] from the tree of knowledge (recognition) of good and evil you shall not eat, otherwise on the day that you eat from it, you shall most certainly die [because of your disobedience]."

—Genesis 2:16–17, AMP

God gave the command directly to Adam, and Eve heard it from him. She knew that she wasn't allowed to eat from that particular tree, so Adam must have communicated this information to her at some point. Unfortunately, the command got distorted, and Eve came to the wrong conclusion. She believed she couldn't even touch the tree, which God never said. It appears that Adam knowingly disobeyed God, but Eve was

---

4   *Merriam Webster*, s.v. "free will," accessed November 21, 2018, https://www.merriam-webster.com/dictionary/free%20will.

deceived. Adam was with her as she ate the fruit and did nothing to correct her interpretation of God's command.

Both Adam and Eve made bad choices that day, but Eve was misled by the devil. Adam willfully and voluntarily made the choice to disobey. The consequences of this wrong choice were huge! They both sinned and failed to heed God's warning, but Adam was held accountable for it. Adam blamed Eve and said that she told him to eat. Even to this day, people say "she/he told me to do it." It's still a lame excuse!

Choices matter! They greatly affect our life and the lives of others. God commands us to do certain things but never overrules our free will. Joshua challenged the Israelites to choose whom they would serve, making it clear that he and his household would serve the Lord. The choice is always ours to make.

Throughout the Old and New Testaments, we find examples of men and women who chose to rejoice. Even without the indwelling of the Holy Spirit, those in the Old Testament knew enough about the character of God to make the choice to rejoice, because they knew He would help them through any difficulty. Listen to what the Prophet Habakkuk said:

Though the fig tree does not blossom
And there is no fruit on the vines,
Though the yield of the olive fails
And the fields produce no food,
Though the flock is cut off from the fold

Choose Joy!

And there are no cattle in the stalls,
Yet I will [choose to] rejoice in the Lord; I will [choose to]
shout in exultation in the [victorious] God of my salvation!
—Habakkuk 3:17–18, AMP

The Lord God is my Strength, my personal bravery, and my invincible army; He makes my feet like hinds' feet and will make me to walk [not to stand still in terror, but to walk] and make [spiritual] progress upon my high places [of trouble, suffering, or responsibility]!

—Habakkuk 3:19, AMPC

King David was a worshipper of God. Many times he made the choice to rejoice in His God, and it brought him through many trials. David made some bad choices and was far from perfect, but God said of him that he was a man after His own heart. Throughout the Psalms, David writes of rejoicing in the Lord and encourages the godly to rejoice:

It's time to sing and shout for joy! Go ahead, all you redeemed ones, do it! Praise him with all you have, for praise looks lovely on the lips of God's lovers. Play the guitar as you lift your praises loaded with thanksgiving. Sing and make joyous music with all you've got inside ... Sing and shout with passion, make a spectacular sound of joy.

—Psalm 33:1–2, 3c, TPT

Pure Joy

"*So go ahead, everyone, and shout out your praises with joy! Break out of the box and let loose with the most joyous sound of praise!*" (Psalm 98:4, TPT). Rejoicing is a choice, and it will release joy.

I know from experience that you can access joy regardless of the situation. I've had to access this joy many times when troubles have come. I know the Holy Spirit resides within me and is the giver of joy, so as I focus on and put my trust in God, joy will result. One time I had to do something extremely difficult for me. I had to come before a judge and explain why my husband needed to be picked up and placed in a mental hospital against his will for his personal safety and protection. I remember feeling fearful, overwhelmed, sad, and guilty. I felt that I had betrayed his trust. My heart was heavy, even though I knew I'd done the right thing. I went home and cried, yet through the tears I began to pray and look to God's Word for comfort and encouragement. Soon I was overcome with great peace and gladness. I knew I had acted out of love and that no matter how hard it was, God was with me and good would come from it. Knowing this filled my heart with joy. Just like Jesus, we can have sorrow and joy simultaneously.

As a youth, David made some choices that would help him through turbulent times in the years ahead. While alone in the fields tending his father's sheep, David learned how to worship and put his trust in God. He developed a lifestyle of joyful praise by rejoicing before the trials, so that when they came, he was able to draw from his relationship with His God. He knew where his help came from: "*My help comes from the Lord, who made heaven and earth*" (Psalm 121:2, NKJV).

Choose Joy!

If we haven't developed a lifestyle of rejoicing when trials come, we'll find it hard to rise above the difficulties. We must choose to rejoice before, during, and after the storm. We need to cultivate joy in our lives. Cultivate, as defined in the Webster Merriam dictionary, means "to foster the growth of" or "to improve by labor, care or study."[5] To grow in our intimacy with the Lord and see joy in our lives, we must, with the aid of the Holy Spirit, choose to foster the growth of joy in our lives. We do this through the study of His Word and time spent in His presence. A wellspring of joy resides within us, but we must decide to embrace and grow in it until it flows in and through us unhindered. We can choose joy over stress, grief, sorrow, tribulations, and adversity. If by our own free will we choose joy, nothing can steal it from us. Jesus said: "*The thief comes only in order to steal and kill and destroy. I came that they may have and enjoy life, and have it in abundance' [to the full, till it overflows]*" (John 10:10, AMP).

The choices we make can have long-term effects and influence future decisions. I've seen it play out in my own life. I received Christ as my Saviour and Lord when I was in my mid-twenties. As a child, I'd gone with a friend to their church and prayed a salvation prayer, but I never took it seriously. When I graduated from high school, I moved from a small town to a large city. I'd done some partying in high school

---

[5] *Merriam Webster*, s.v. "cultivate," accessed November 21, 2018, https://www.merriam-webster.com/dictionary/cultivate.

and spent a lot of time listening to rock and roll music, but I became even more involved in that lifestyle once I left home. I got into drugs as well.

I really loved listening to music; I owned over a hundred records. I sang along but never consciously paid attention to the lyrics. Shortly after I got saved, I felt led to read the words in the songs. I was shocked by what they talked of—suicide, murder, sex, parties, drinking, broken relationships, and other negative things. I took those records, smashed them, and threw them in the garbage. I still loved music, so I began to collect and listen to Christian music, especially praise and worship songs. I soon realized how encouraging and uplifting the music was and how I felt a strong presence of the Lord every time I listened to it. The non-Christian music I used to listen to never uplifted me. I chose to obey the leading of the Holy Spirit by reading the words of the songs and then switching to Christian music to help me grow close to God and discover the benefits of a lifestyle of rejoicing. One of those benefits was the joy it brought to me, making it easier to deal with the cares and difficulties of life. It set me up to rejoice through all the battles I've faced over the years.

To this day, there's nothing I enjoy more than rejoicing in the Lord and being full of His joy. I love to play worship music in my home, as it creates a peaceful, joyful atmosphere. The decisions I made early in my Christian life made it easier to obey the Lord when a major crisis came. In the midst of the trials I faced in the life and death of my husband, I knew that even though I felt shocked and overwhelmed with emotion, the Holy Spirit was telling me to praise God. I understood that I could praise my way through, and if I made the choice to rejoice, joy would come. My friend and I praised and rejoiced with grateful hearts that victory over death had been won for my husband. He was where we all longed to be—in the physical presence of the Lord. God's grace carried me, and His love, joy, and peace bubbled up inside. The joy of the Lord became my strength, all because I chose to obey!

Once we arrived back in Canada after learning of my husband's death, we had to make a connecting flight from Calgary to our home city of Saskatoon. God set this up, as our pastor and his wife, Cathy, were returning from another city and were booked on the same connecting flight. They met us as we got off the first plane, and Cathy said to me later that when we walked off that plane, we had smiles on our faces and were so joyful. We chose to rejoice, and it showed in the midst of a very chaotic situation. Right choices make all the difference!

How well we overcome tragedy has everything to do with our choices—not just those you make during the storm, but the ones you make before any difficulty even comes. If you haven't learned to praise during good times, it will be hard to push yourself to do so when troubles arise. The Bible tells us in Proverbs: "*Every word of God proves true ...*" (Proverbs 30:5a, ESV). If we obey the Word and follow its commands, we'll experience the results of that choice: "*Always be joyful. Never stop praying. Be thankful in all circumstances, for this is God's will for you who belong to Christ Jesus*" (1 Thessalonians 5:16–18, NLT); "*I will bless the Lord at all times; His praise shall continually be in my mouth*" (Psalm 34:1,

NKJV). To continually bless the Lord is to say something good about the Lord all the time. Choose to be glad, and you won't be sad! Choose to be glad, and you won't be mad!

As Christians, we aren't exempt from trouble, but we do have a choice in how we handle it. Joy is a fruit of the Spirit that grows in our hearts as we grow in Him. When we choose to rejoice, it's released from our hearts. You can't experience the joy that comes from the Holy Spirit unless your spirit is alive to God. The best choice any human being can make is to accept Christ as their Saviour and Lord. This impacts those around them, especially their children and grandchildren. The decision to receive Christ's salvation is an individual choice, but we can encourage and influence others by sharing with them the plan of salvation. When we choose to live for Christ, we choose eternal life and set the stage for those who come after us to do the same. Once we have God's life living on the inside, we can choose to access all that God has for us, including joy.

But only if you live obediently to God, your God, and keep the commandments and regulations written in this Book of Revelation. Nothing halfhearted here; you must return to God, your God, totally, heart and soul, holding nothing back. This commandment that I'm commanding you today isn't too much for you, it's not out of your reach. It's not on a high mountain—you don't have to get mountaineers to climb the peak and bring it down to your level and explain it before you can live it. And it's not across the ocean—you don't have to send sailors out to get it, bring it back, and then explain it before you can live it. No. The word is right here and now—as near as the tongue in your mouth, as near as the heart in your chest. Just do it! Look at what I've done for you today: I've placed in front of you Life and Good Death and Evil. And I command you today: Love God, your God. Walk in his ways. Keep his commandments, regulations, and rules so that you will live, really live, live exuberantly, blessed by God...

—Deuteronomy 30:10-16a, MSG

I call Heaven and Earth to witness against you today: I place before you Life and Death, Blessing and Curse. Choose life so that you and your children will live. And love God, your God, listening obediently to him, firmly embracing him. Oh yes, he is life itself...

—Deuteronomy 30:19–20a, MSG

Jesus talks of the joy that comes from Him alone, even during times of great sorrow, such as the disciples experienced when He was taken from them. Jesus told them that they would have joy because of the understanding that one day they would see Him again in heaven. He explained that this joy would never be taken from them, for joy is eternal:

When a woman gives birth, she has a hard time, there's no getting around it. But when the baby is born, there is joy in the birth. This new life in the world wipes out memory of the pain. The sadness you have right now is similar to that pain, but the coming joy is also similar. When I see you again, you'll be full of joy, and it will be a joy that no one can rob from you ...

—John 16:21–22, MSG

Jesus also told them to ask in His name, and their joy would be full. When we choose to come to the Father and ask for His help in Jesus' name, we are filled with joy.

For here is eternal truth: When that time comes you won't need to ask me for anything, but instead you will go directly to the Father and ask him for anything you desire and he will give it to you, because of your relationship with me. Until now you've not been bold enough to ask the Father for a single thing in my name, but now you can ask, and keep on asking him! And you can be sure that you'll receive what you ask for, and your joy will have no limits!

—John 16:23–24, TPT

As believers in Christ, we should choose to live a life overflowing with joy!

We constantly make decisions, even though we aren't always aware of it. Some choices are made unconsciously or out of habit, and other times they're made consciously. As we are Spirit-led, we make more right choices. We'll still make mistakes and at times unwise decisions, as only God is perfect and good all the time. The more Christ-like we become, the fewer wrong choices we make. It's important to give the Holy Spirit permission to direct us, and He will help us make good choices. Choosing to rejoice always and be filled with joy is being wise.

As we continually surrender our lives to the Lord, giving our time, attention, and worship to Him, the more we walk in wisdom. When we make the choice for Christ, we put ourselves in a position to be led by His Spirit. The Holy Spirit is the very presence of God on the earth, and He abides with us. He enables us to endure and overcome any hardship, because the Lord's strength resides in us, infusing us with His joy. No matter the persecution, trials, or afflictions that come our way, we can choose to live a joy-filled life.

If we decide to walk according to the flesh, we choose to sin, being led by the lusts of the flesh. This is what happened to Adam and Eve. They made a bad choice to eat the fruit, according to the desires of their flesh, and sin came into the world. When we choose to walk in the Spirit, we allow the fruits of the Spirit to manifest in our lives, one of which is joy.

As you yield freely and fully to the dynamic life and power of the Holy Spirit, you will abandon the cravings of your self-life. For your self-life craves the things that offend the Holy Spirit and hinder him from living free within you! And the Holy Spirit's intense cravings hinder your old self-life from dominating you! So then, the two incompatible and conflicting forces within you are your self-life of the flesh and the new creation life of the Spirit. But when you are brought into full freedom of the Spirit of grace, you will no longer be living under the domination of the law, but soaring above it!

The cravings of the self-life are obvious: Sexual immorality, lustful thoughts, pornography, chasing after things instead of God, manipulating others, hatred of those who get in your way, senseless arguments, resentment when others are favored, temper tantrums, angry quarrels, only thinking of yourself, being in love with your own opinions, being envious of the blessings of others, murder, uncontrolled addictions, wild parties, and all other similar behavior. Haven't I already warned you that those who use their "freedom" for these things will not inherit the kingdom realm of God! But the fruit produced by the Holy Spirit within you is divine love in all its varied expressions: Joy that overflows, peace that subdues, patience that endures, kindness in action, a life full of virtue, faith that prevails, gentleness of heart and strength of spirit. Never set the law above these qualities, for they are meant to be limitless. Keep in mind that we who belong to Jesus, the Anointed One, have already experienced crucifixion. For everything connected with our self-life was put to death on the cross and crucified with Messiah. We must live in the Holy Spirit and follow after him.

—Galatians 5:16-25, TPT

Making right choices is a continual battle in the mind. By choice we can cast down every thought that is contrary to the Word of God. We can think in a Christ-like manner, allowing the Holy Spirit to fill our minds with His thoughts:

Choose Joy!

We can demolish every deceptive fantasy that opposes God and break through every arrogant attitude that is raised up in defiance of the true knowledge of God. We capture, like prisoners of war, every thought and insist that it bow in obedience to the Anointed One.

—2 Corinthians 10:5, TPT

Choose to believe the truth of God's Word. The Word tells us to rejoice at all times! We can choose joy.

WHAT IS REAL JOY?
Chapter Three

"But the fruit of the Spirit is ... joy ... "

—Galatians 5:22

What is real joy? It's much more than a feeling of contentment. It's not the emotion of being glad rather than being sad or mad, and it's not something that comes and goes depending on a person's mood or situation. It's steady, continuous, and supernatural. It's the very essence of who God is, the very nature of heaven shining through on earth. It's not something you can fake or make up. It's genuine and comes from the very heart of God.

Joy originates with our Heavenly Father. It's a character trait of the Father displayed through the Holy Spirit, and it acts as an outward sign that the Holy Spirit is abiding and operating in and through us. It's only available to those whose spirits have been made alive to God through their faith in Christ Jesus.

Mother Theresa once said: "Joy is prayer—Joy is strength—Joy is love—joy is a net of love by which you can catch souls. God loves a cheerful giver. She gives most who gives with joy. The best way to show our gratitude to God and the people is to accept everything with joy. A joyful heart is the inevitable result of a heart burning with love. Never let anything so fill you with sorrow as to make you forget the joy of the Christ risen."[6]

The Merriam Webster dictionary defines happiness as "a pleasurable or satisfying experience."[7] Happiness is a feeling we sense when everything is going well, but the feeling is fleeting. There one minute, gone the next! Joy is anchored in the love of God and remains even when it appears that everything around us is falling apart. Nothing can remove it from us. Happiness can disappear the moment something unforeseen takes place. Joy does affect our emotions—it feels pleasurable and satisfying—but it's constant and doesn't disappear when something goes wrong. Joy is unaffected by circumstances and remains steadfast in the midst of chaos.

Joy is a state of being that exists no matter the situation, whereas feelings of happiness, gladness, or cheerfulness arise when our circumstances are good. Feelings derived from our perspective of a situation. If we believe someone dislikes us or talks badly about us, it arouses emotions of sadness or anger. Real joy isn't a feeling or emotion dependant upon what others say or think.

---

[6] "Mother Teresa Quotations," Memorable Quotations, accessed May 12, 2018, http://www.memorablequotations.com/mother.htm.

[7] *Merriam-Webster*, s.v. "happiness," accessed November 18, 2018, https://www.merriam-webster.com/dictionary/happiness.

Pure Joy

Blessed [morally courageous and spiritually alive with life-joy in God's goodness] are you when people insult you and persecute you, and falsely say all kinds of evil things against you because of [your association with] Me. Be glad and exceedingly joyful, for your reward in heaven is great [absolutely inexhaustible]; for in this same way they persecuted the prophets who were before you.

—Matthew 5:11–12, AMP

As young Christians, we weren't always wise in the way we spoke to our families about our new faith in Christ. They were quite upset with us on several occasions, especially my husband's family. Not long before we were married, Clarence got into a disagreement with his dad and basically told him he was going to hell if he didn't repent and receive Christ as his Saviour. He was enthusiastic about what he believed, but he didn't use wisdom when speaking with his father. (He later learned to approach his dad in a different way and eventually led him to the Lord.)

His dad was so angry with him that he kicked him out of the house and told him to never come back. I remember getting a phone call to come and pick him up. Clarence's sister and I were living in Yorkton, a city about an hour away from the farm. Cecilia and I drove into the yard to get Clarence, who was sitting on the front step of the house with his suitcase, waiting for us.

What Is Real Joy?

As we drove in, we starting laughing. Clarence came to the truck with a big smile on his face and said, "All I did was tell him he needed to get saved or he'd go to hell."

"Well," I said, "that may be true, but I don't think it was quite the right way to say it. The Bible does say we'll be persecuted for our faith, though."

The three of us started rejoicing and declaring salvation over our families, and we were filled with overflowing joy and laughter.

Emotions are part of our human nature, but joy is different—it comes from God's Spirit. Joy is a strong foundation in our spiritual life that reinforces healthy emotions and attitudes. In the world, joy and happiness are synonymous, but natural joy differs from spiritual joy. The joy that comes from the Lord isn't based on the absence of difficulties but on the truth of God's Word. When we don't allow joy to flow, we suppress the Holy Spirit in our lives: "*Don't hold the Spirit back*" (1 Thessalonians 5:19, FBV).

Love is the first fruit mentioned in the list of fruits of the Spirit in Galatians 5. I believe this is because God is love, and all the other fruits are rooted in love. Love produces seeds that grow into joy, peace, patience, kindness, goodness, faithfulness, gentleness, and self-control. Joy is produced out of God's love for us. We are created in the image of God—in love!

The fruit in our lives comes out of our relationship with the Lord. When we abide in the vine, we produce much fruit, and joy will abound.

Pure Joy

Live in me, and I will live in you. A branch cannot produce any fruit by itself. It has to stay attached to the vine. In the same way, you cannot produce fruit unless you live in me. I am the vine. You are the branches. Those who live in me while I live in them will produce a lot of fruit. But you can't produce anything without me.

—John 15:4–5, GW

The Greek word for joy in Galatians 5 is *chara*, which means "gladness or delight." The Psalmist writes: "*Take delight in the Lord, and he will give you the desires of your heart*" (Psalm 37:4). Take joy in the Lord, and your heart's desire will be for more of Him ... more joy! Joy produces joy!

Rejoice is a verb for joy. Rejoicing is joy in action! When we rejoice, we put joy on display. We have much to rejoice about. The Lord is always full of joy, and He rejoices over us. Paul serves as a great example; he rejoiced no matter what came his way, and we should do likewise. The Prophet Zephaniah states: "*For the Lord your God is living among you. He is a mighty savior. He will take delight in you with gladness. With his love, he will calm all your fears. He will rejoice over you with joyful songs*" (Zephaniah 3:17, NLT).

Joy acts as an antidote for negative emotions, attitudes, and circumstances. The Collins English dictionary defines antidote as "anything that works against an evil or unwanted condition."[8] The English Oxford Living dictionary defines it as "Something that counteracts an unpleasant feeling or situation."[9] Grief, sorrow, hopelessness, fear, worry, stress, anxiety, and depression drain us of physical and mental strength, but joy energizes us spiritually and physically: "*A joyful, cheerful heart brings healing to both body and soul ...*" (Proverbs 17:22, TPT); "*Anxious fear brings depression ...*" (Proverbs 12:25a, TPT).

Negative feelings are natural human emotions; however, joy is a spiritual attribute of our Heavenly Father that manifests in our lives through the Holy Spirit.

---

[8] *Collins*, s.v. "antidote," accessed November 18, 2018, https://www.collinsdictionary.com/dictionary/english/antidote.

[9] *English Oxford Living Dictionaries*, s.v. "antidote," accessed November 9, 2018, https://en.oxforddictionaries.com/definition/antidote.

FULLNESS OF JOY
Chapter Four

> *"You make the path of life known to me. In your presence there is complete joy."*
>
> —Acts 2:28, GW

God wants us to live life to the fullest and enjoy every day. We will never experience complete joy apart from Christ, as He is the source of all joy. Have you ever heard someone say "She/he completes me"? We are incomplete without God. He completes us: "*For he is the complete fullness of deity living in human form. And our own completeness is now found in him. We are completely filled with God as Christ's fullness overflows with in us ...*" (Colossians 2:9–10a, TPT).

We will only be satisfied when we live a life dominated by the Holy Spirit. In His presence, we find fulfillment. The Word of God says to be filled with the Holy Spirit. When we're filled with the Spirit of God, we're full of joy. We are also told to enter His gates with thanksgiving and His courts with praise (Psalm 100:4). Grateful rejoicing is the entrance point to His presence, as it gives us access to the Holy Spirit, God's presence on this earth. Rejoicing results in overflowing joy. The Collins English dictionary explains "overflowing" this way:

"If someone is overflowing with a feeling or if the feeling overflows, the person is experiencing it very strongly and shows this in their behavior."[10]

The Lord doesn't want us to put a lid on the Holy Spirit but to be so full of joy that it flows out of us like a river in flood stage. On the Day of Pentecost when the Holy Spirit came, they were so filled with the Holy Spirit that it spilled out of them, and they behaved as though they were drunk. The Lord wants us to shine forth, filled to capacity with the things of the Spirit. In Ephesians 4, Paul tells the Ephesians to be kind to each other and to forgive in the same way God in Christ forgave them. In the next chapter, he instructs them to be imitators of Christ and walk in love. In verse eight, Paul says to walk in the light of the Lord and have nothing to do with the works of darkness, and in verse eighteen He tells them to be filled with the Spirit.

To experience fullness of joy, we must be kind, forgiving, loving, and filled with the Spirit. We are to imitate Jesus Christ, who was filled with the Spirit throughout His earthly life. If He needed to be filled with the Holy Spirit, how much more do we! We need to heed Paul's words: "*Imitate God, therefore, in everything you do, because you are his dear children. Live a life filled with love, following the example of Christ ...*" (Ephesians 5:1–2a, NLT); "*For once you were full of darkness, but now you have light from*

---

[10] *Collins*, s.v. "overflowing," accessed November 18, 2018, https://www.collinsdictionary.com/dictionary/english/overflowing.

the Lord. So live as people of light! For this light within you produces only what is good and right and true" (Ephesians 5:8–9, NLT).

> *And don't get drunk with wine, which is rebellion; instead be filled with the fullness of the Holy Spirit. And your hearts will overflow with a joyful song to the Lord Jehovah. Keep speaking to each other with words of Scripture, singing the Psalms with praises and spontaneous songs given by the Spirit!*
> —Ephesians 5:18–19, TPT

When my children were young, the Lord said to me: "Be what you want your children to be." Children are imitators. If you want them to be worshippers, be a worshipper. Show love to all people, and they will do the same. If you want them to be servers, show them by serving. It's the same with joy or having a positive outlook on life. If you're joyful and positive, they will copy you and learn to be that way. If you're always negative, grumbling, and unhappy, they'll become like you. All people are products of their environment, from what they observe and experience from day to day. If you're a cheerful person, they will watch and learn how to be joyful, have fun, and enjoy life. We want to be an example so that people will pattern their lives after us as we follow Christ. Paul said, "*Imitate me, just as I imitate Christ*" (1 Corinthians 11:1, CEB). The Passion Translation says it this way: "*I want you to pattern your lives after me, just as I pattern mine after Christ*" (TPT).

We are to be containers of joy that continually bubble over. He fills us up so that we can give it away. He has given us everything that pertains to life and godliness, including joy: "*Jesus has the power of God, by which he has given us everything we need to live and serve God. We have these things because we know him. Jesus called us by his glory and goodness*" (2 Peter 1:3, NCV). Joy is part of our spiritual DNA. We don't overflow with joy by pursuing it but by chasing after the Joy Giver. We find ourselves full of gladness as we serve the Lord and others. When people see us enjoying life as we live and serve God, they will desire the joy we have. It will become irresistible, and they will do whatever is necessary to receive it.

Joy is contagious! "Contagious" as defined by the English Oxford dictionary means "(of an emotion, feeling or attitude) likely to spread to and affect others."[11] The Merriam-Webster dictionary defines "contagious" as "exciting similar emotions or conduct in others; contagious enthusiasm, contagious laughter."[12] Yourdictionary.com defines it as, "Spreading or tending to spread from one to another; infectious: a contagious smile."[13]

Yes, to have true, lasting joy we must receive Jesus as our Lord and Saviour—the Joy Giver—but our good attitude will rub off on others, and they will learn to be positive, happy

---

11 *English Oxford Living Dictionaries*, s.v. "contagious," accessed May 12, 2018, https://en.oxforddictionaries.com/definition/courageous.

12 *Merriam Webster*, s.v. "contagious," accessed November 22, 2018, https://www.merriam-webster.com/dictionary/contagious.

13 *Yourdictionary.com*, s.v. "contagious," accessed May 12, 2018, http://www.yourdictionary.com/contagious?direct_search_result=yes.

people just from being around us. Add Jesus into the mix, and you have the remedy to fight all negativity and live a pure, joy-filled life. When we remain joyful through difficult times, others notice and hunger for what we have.

As a new Christian, I began attending a church in a small town near my fiancé's farm. An evangelist named Anna attended there as well. I was amazed by and drawn to her zest for life; she radiated with love and joy. She had a contagious smile, and her whole face lit up when she smiled. If you were feeling down, you couldn't stay miserable for long when in her presence. She was the most joyful, content person I'd ever met. She was always positive, uplifting, and encouraging with her words, attitude, and actions. She had a profound impact on my life.

Anna loved to praise the Lord and had recorded several country gospel songs, many that she'd written herself. I didn't particularly like listening to that genre of music, and her singing voice wasn't all that great, but there was such an anointing when she sang and played her guitar. She belted out those songs with such energy, enthusiasm, and gladness of heart that it didn't matter if her voice wasn't the best. It sounded wonderful to God, and I learned from her that I could sing and worship the Lord with all my heart. It didn't matter what it sounded like; it was beautiful to Him. When I praised my God in this manner, overwhelming joy resulted.

Anna impacted my life all those years ago, and I believe she still influences people today. She is a catalyst for joy. God wants us to be catalyst for joy! Here are three definitions for "catalyst" taken for different sources:

1. Dictionary.com: "a person whose talk, enthusiasm, or energy causes others to be more friendly, enthusiastic, or energetic."[14]
2. Collins English dictionary: "a person or thing that causes a change."[15]
3. Yourdictionary.com: "someone or something that encourages progress or change."[16]

Anna was a modern-day Barnabas. Barnabas is a good biblical example of a catalyst. His name means "son of encouragement," and he was an encourager and a joy-filled person. Acts 11 outlines the story of Barnabas being sent to Antioch by the church in Jerusalem upon hearing that many non-Jews were receiving Christ as their Lord and Saviour.

The news about this reached the church in Jerusalem, so they sent Barnabas to Antioch. When he arrived and saw how God had blessed the people, he was glad and urged them all to be faithful and true to the Lord with all their hearts.

---

[14] *Dictionary.com*, s.v. "catalyst," accessed November 9, 2018, https://www.dictionary.com/browse/catalyst.

[15] *Collins*, s.v. "catalyst," accessed November 18, 2018, https://www.collinsdictionary.com/dictionary/english/catalyst.

[16] *Yourdictionary.com*, s.v. "catalyst," accessed November 9, 2018, http://www.yourdictionary.com/catalyst?direct_search_result=yes.

Pure Joy

Barnabas was a good man, full of the Holy Spirit and faith, and many people were brought to the Lord.

—Acts 11:22–24, CEB

I love being a catalyst for joy. On many occasions, joy has overcome me, and others have caught that Spirit of joy. Before I was married to Clarence, his sister Cecilia and I were visiting an older neighbour, Myrna, who lived on a farm next to theirs. Myrna told us that she was going to sing the next day at a relative's wedding, and her husband was going to play the organ. She didn't want to sing alone, so she asked Cecilia if she'd sing with her. Cecilia said she would sing if I would, and I told her I would sing if Clarence would.

The next day at the wedding, we were asked to stand at the back of the church, while the organ was at the front. It was a weird set up. When the bride entered, she was crying, and it didn't seem like happy tears. A lot of the guests were crying as well. Clarence whispered to me, "What is this, a shotgun wedding?"

When the time came to sing the first song, Myrna handed us each a hymnal and told us what page to turn to. With the organ playing at the front, we began to sing. Part way through the song, I stopped singing. All I remember is hearing Clarence singing—he was tone deaf. It sounded so bad, I burst into laughter! Myrna seemed oblivious to it all, but not Cecilia. She was annoyed with me and kept telling me to stop laughing.

Fullness of Joy

"God has a sense of humour," I said. "I think we're here to bring some life and joy to this very sad wedding. Listen to your brother sing, because he's awful."

"No way," she replied. "I'm not doing that, and don't laugh ... it's very rude."

A few minutes later, the choir began to sing another hymn. We joined in, and I was trying my hardest not to laugh, but it was just so hilarious listening to Clarence sing. Cecilia's curiosity got the better of her, and she stopped to listen to her brother. She began laughing hysterically. Both of us were laughing so hard, we ended up rolling around on the floor. It looked more like a revival meeting than a wedding. It was contagious and brought much joy to the wedding. Everyone was laughing, and even thirty years later as I tell this story, I start laughing. Laughter is a by-product, or result, of joy.

When believers in Christ live a joy-filled life, they encourage others to make the necessary changes in their lives to obtain lasting joy. Joy is a motivator for change. When we live a life of complete joy, others will be drawn to the giver of joy, who abides with us.

KEYS TO JOY—PART ONE
Chapter Five

"Enter into His gates with thanksgiving,
And into His courts with praise.
Be thankful to Him, and bless His name."

—Psalm 100:4, NKJV

Joy abides in our recreated spirit, but it will lay dormant within us unless we act and do what's necessary to access it. It comes to us in seed form and will only grow into mature fruit as we spend time in the presence of the Lord and develop a close, intimate relationship with Him. We must be continually filled with the Holy Spirit to ensure enduring joy in our lives. I have identified seven keys from studying and cultivating joy in my own life. They are all interchangeable; you can't have one without the other. They go hand-in-hand. The culmination of all these keys will bring us fulfillment and complete joy. These seven access points are: thankfulness, praise, prayer, God's Word, serving, sharing Jesus/salvation, and living by faith.

Keys to Joy—Part One

Thankfulness

Thankfulness is the gateway to joy. Rejoicing, or praising the Lord, is joy in action. The psalmist tells us in Psalm 100:4 to enter His gates with thanksgiving and His courts with praise. We can't praise or rejoice without first being thankful. Paul admonishes us to be thankful: "*in everything give thanks; for this is the will of God in Christ Jesus for you*" (1 Thessalonians 5:18, NKJV). Joy comes when we rejoice with a thankful heart, and we have much to be thankful for! We will never be able to consider it all joy if we're not grateful in the difficult times. Being thankful is a command. When we show gratitude to the Lord in the midst of the storm, we're not giving Him thanks for the trial but for His goodness. God isn't responsible for the negative circumstances that arise in our lives. He can, however, work good through the most horrible of situations, and for that we can always be thankful.

In 1 Thessalonians 5:16, we're commanded to rejoice always. In verse eighteen, we're told to give thanks in everything. We won't be able to rejoice continually if we don't learn to be thankful in all things. Joy comes from the indwelling of the Holy Spirit. It's an inner contentment that arises within us as we learn to develop a lifestyle of thankfulness. It's not that hard to be thankful when you understand that God is good and that He's always with us and in control of every situation.

One winter many years ago, the city of Saskatoon changed to a different company to remove snow from the streets. Those who live in the city know that the residential side streets don't get ploughed out a lot, but the main streets always do. One day a friend and I were driving on Idylwyld, the main road through the city, when I slammed on my brakes, losing control of the car. The road hadn't been ploughed well, and it still had ruts. We spun around three times in heavy traffic but didn't hit any cars. We finally stopped on top of a six-foot snow bank in the median between the traffic. It all happened so fast, when I looked out the window and saw our location, I was in awe. I asked my friend if she was okay. She said that she was but commented that the car looked a little smashed up.

"Well, thank the Lord we aren't hurt," I responded. "We didn't smash into any other vehicles, and my car can be fixed."

As we sat on that mound of snow, joy began to bubble up in us, and we began to laugh. "How did we get up here?" I asked. "God is so good; our angels must have put the car here." There were no tire marks leading up the snow bank, like there should have been. We sat in the car laughing until the police showed up. The officer got out of the car and walked up the snow bank and asked if we were okay. We told him we were fine. He shook his head and asked, "How in the world did you end up here?"

I continued to laugh and said, "I have no idea other than I have angels watching out for me."

"Well, if you're okay, I'll call a tow truck and get you off of here."

A few minutes later, the tow trunk came and pulled us off the snow bank, and away we went.

Keys to Joy—Part One

When we're thankful and acknowledge the Lord in these situations, without getting upset, joy results. I knew my husband would be thankful that we were okay, but I knew he wasn't going to be too impressed with the damage to our vehicle. But I didn't really care. I was just glad that we were safe and that our angels took care of us. Thankfulness always brings joy.

Daniel is a good example in the Old Testament of someone who gave thanks in all circumstances. He was faced with a very difficult situation. A new law decreed that if anyone prayed to any god or person other than the king, they would be thrown into the lions' den. Upon hearing about the new law, Daniel stood firm.

> *When Daniel learned that the decree had been signed and posted, he continued to pray just as he had always done. His house had windows in the upstairs that opened toward Jerusalem. Three times a day he knelt there in prayer, thanking and praising God.*
>
> —Daniel 6:10, MSG

Daniel was thrown into a den of hungry lions because he disobeyed the law. God took care of Daniel and shut the lions' mouths. In the morning, the king came to see if Daniel was okay. No harm had come to Daniel, because he trusted in his God and thanked, prayed, and praised Him in spite of the life-threatening situation. When the king discovered that Daniel hadn't been hurt in any way, he was overjoyed. Being thankful in everything will not only bring joy to the person offering thanks, but to others as well as they observe how God takes care of those who show gratitude no matter what.

> *Then the king waxed exceedingly glad and commanded that Daniel should be taken up out of the den. So Daniel was taken up out of the den, and no hurt of any kind was found on him because he believed (relied on, adhered to, and trusted in) his God.*
>
> —Daniel 6:23, AMPC

The Bible is full of examples of people who learned to live a life of thankfulness. The psalmist David wrote several psalms filled with thanksgiving and rejoicing. The apostle Paul was imprisoned in Rome, in chains, not knowing when the Roman soldiers might come to get him to execute him for his beliefs. He was wrongly incarcerated, all alone, and mistreated … but he wrote to several of the churches, encouraging them to be thankful and rejoice in everything. If anyone had a reason to grumble and complain, it was Paul. But he had learned to cultivate thankfulness in his life and to be content in whatever situation he found himself.

Jesus is the greatest example of one who knew how to be grateful. In several situations, He gave thanks. He gave thanks before He raised his friend Lazarus from the dead, before the disciples handed out the loaves and fishes, and during the Passover supper with His disciples, just to name a few.

Keys to Joy—Part One

Corrie Ten Boom in her book *The Hiding Place* tells the story of how her sister, Betsie, challenged her while they were being held in the Ravensbruck concentration camp for hiding Jews in their home. She dared Corrie to give thanks in all circumstances (1 Thessalonians 5:18). They lived in horrible conditions. Fleas bit them continually, but Corrie and her sister gave thanks for their awful conditions, including the fleas. They noticed that the guards never came near their barracks, so they began to hold worship services in the dormitory. Many of the women came to Christ. They couldn't understand why the guards never came around until one day they needed a supervisor to settle a dispute, but she refused to come because of the fleas. Those terrible flees that made their lives almost unbearable were used by God to enable Corrie and Betsie to share the gospel with many women, saving them from an eternal hell worse than anything they experienced in the camp. Many of those women, including Betsie, died in that place but are in heaven today because those two sisters chose to sacrificially thank God in the midst of horrific circumstances. The result of their decision to give thanks was joy. Corrie Ten Boom once said: "When we are powerless to do a thing, it is a great joy that we can come and step inside the ability of Jesus."[17]

---

[17] "Corrie ten Boom Quotes," goodreads, accessed August 5, 2018, https://www.goodreads.com/author/quotes/102203.Corrie_ten_Boom.

Being thankful is a discipline that we must cultivate in our lives if we want to grow in and experience more joy.

> *Let the peace of Christ keep you in tune with each other, in step with each other. None of this going off and doing your own thing. And cultivate thankfulness. Let the Word of Christ—the Message—have the run of the house. Give it plenty of room in your lives. Instruct and direct one another using good common sense. And sing, sing your hearts out to God! Let every detail in your lives—words, actions, whatever—be done in the name of the Master, Jesus, thanking God the Father every step of the way.*
>
> —Colossians 3:15–17, MSG

Praise

Praise and thanksgiving are interconnected, like Siamese twins: unique, different, yet the same. Throughout scripture when praise is mentioned, thanksgiving is spoken of as well.

The Bible refers to both praise and thanksgiving as a sacrifice. In Yourdictionary.com, the definition of sacrifice is "an offering or giving up of something."[18] The Merriam Webster dictionary states that it's "an act of offering to a deity something

---

18 *Yourdictionary.com*, s.v. "sacrifice," accessed November 22, 2018, https://www.yourdictionary.com/sacrifice?direct_search_result=yes.

Keys to Joy—Part One

precious."[19] Throughout the Word of God, we're told to offer sacrifices of praise. The writer of Hebrews says, "*So we no longer offer up a steady stream of blood sacrifices, but through Jesus, we will offer up to God a steady stream of praise sacrifices—these are 'the lambs' we offer from our lips that celebrate his name!*" (Hebrews 13:15, TPT). We give our praise to God and get joy in return, "... *pressed down, shaken together, and running over* ..." (Luke 6:38).

For the Israelites, praise was a lifestyle they were commanded by God to live out. In the Book of Nehemiah, after rebuilding the wall of Jerusalem, Nehemiah dedicated it to the Lord: "*That day many sacrifices were offered, and the people were full of joy because God had made them very happy. The women and children joined in the celebration, and the noise they all made could be heard for miles*" (Nehemiah 12:43, GNT).

You can't praise and not rejoice, and you won't rejoice without praising. Our joy will increase the more we praise and thank Him. I've experienced this in my own life many times. Praising is like watering the fruit of joy. The more we praise, the more joy is produced.

Praise needs to become habitual. When we develop a lifestyle of praise, it's easier to obey, even in the most difficult of times. The greater and more consistent our praise life, the more joyful we'll become. Praise sets our focus on God and takes it off ourselves. It brings us into the courts of our King, into His

---

19   *Merriam Webster*, s.v. "sacrifice," accessed November 22, 2018, https://www.merriam-webster.com/dictionary/sacrifice.

very presence. In His presence our spirits are refreshed and renewed, resulting in a greater enjoyment of life. Whenever I find myself in a tough place and feelings of discontent try to surface, I lift my hands, raise my voice, and start praising my God. As I do, joy and gladness flood my whole being, spirit, soul, and body.

> *Because your loving kindness is better than life,*
> *My lips will praise You.*
> *Thus I will bless you while I live;*
> *I will lift up my hands in Your name.*
> *My soul shall be satisfied as with marrow and fatness,*
> *And my mouth shall praise You with joyful lips.*
> —Psalm 63:3–5, NKJV

Praise is a declaration of our faith; it's an act of obedience that sets us on a course to exponential joy. Praise from a heart of thankfulness is always joyful! I recall two occasions when praise brought such joy. I was pregnant with my second daughter, Brittney, almost twenty-nine years ago. A few weeks before she was due, the doctor discovered that she was in a breech position. It wasn't a footling breech, and I hadn't had any problems with the birth of my first child, so the doctor said I could give birth naturally.

I was told to go to the hospital at the first sign of labour, as my first labour was only five hours long. At the hospital they put me into a bed and hooked me up to a monitor, as they routinely do. Two student nurses in the room looked concerned.

My husband said, "You've probably witnessed some difficult births, but just stick around here and you'll experience an enjoyable birth. My wife is the calmest person around, and her first birth was easy and fast."

One of the nurses asked for the prenatal papers, and when they discovered that my daughter was going to be a breech birth, they began to panic. They told the nurse on duty, and soon everyone began to shout to get the operating room ready in case I needed a C-section. I starting laughing and said, "You're all hilarious; everything will be fine."

"Yes," my husband agreed, "we're Christians, and God's got this under control. Just stay calm!"

I smiled and laughed at their antics. I had total peace and confidence that everything would be fine, and joy was bubbling up inside me. Everything went extremely well. After my daughter was born, the doctor told me that she fell out quite easily. Even now I smile and sense joy rising and want to laugh when I think about how they were so concerned while we were so calm, watching it all unfold. God will give you joy for any situation. It's a matter of trust and knowing that He's in control.

The other situation took place after my husband's death. I spent most of my time praising the Lord. It never failed to take my focus off myself and put it onto Him. After I arrived home from Kenya, Pastor Randall said, "I think we should have a praise night." I remember that evening well. We worshipped and celebrated with family, close friends, and church family. There was great joy and thanksgiving in my heart knowing that death had lost its sting, and Clarence had won the victory over death. The enemy had to come to steal, kill, and destroy through that horrendous tragedy, but Jesus brought us life, and that more abundantly.

My son Jared got up that evening and said something that I'll never forget: "I choose to be a victor, not a victim." Those words caused such joy to flood my heart. I remember going home to our acreage that night with my son, both of us rejoicing and talking about how good God was. It was the first time I'd entered our house since Clarence's death, as I'd stayed for a few days with my pastor and his wife. Joy and peace overwhelmed us when we walked in the door. Joy is rejoicing in action, and it will turn your mourning into dancing.

Our praises can become ritualistic because they're expected of us, but true praise comes from the heart. God is worthy of all honour, glory, and praise. Jesus said that if we don't praise Him, the rocks will:

As soon as He was approaching [Jerusalem], near the descent of the Mount of Olives, the entire multitude of the disciples [all those who were or claimed to be His followers] began praising God [adoring Him enthusiastically and] joyfully with loud voices for all the miracles and works of power that they had seen, shouting, "Blessed (celebrated, praised) is THE KING WHO COMES IN THE NAME OF THE LORD! Peace in heaven and glory (majesty, splendor) in the highest [heaven]!" Some of the Pharisees from the crowd said to Him, "Teacher rebuke Your disciples [for shouting

Keys to Joy—Part One

these Messianic praises]." Jesus replied, "I tell you, if these [people] keep silent, the stones will cry out [in praise]!"
—Luke 19:37–40, AMP

When I visited Indonesia and Kenya, I discovered that I knew little about what it meant to abandon oneself to God in praise. I've been to some remote villages in both Kenya and Indonesia where the people are very poor and have little in the way of material blessings, yet they have such a great love for the Lord and are very rich in spirit. They are some of the most thankful, praising, and joy-filled people I've ever had the pleasure of meeting. Many, especially in Kenya, are so poor, they don't even own a Bible.

People in Canada donated money so that we could buy Bibles and sheep to give to the villagers in Kenya. We gave out the Bibles during a Sunday service. The pastor decided who in the congregation should receive a Bible. They called their name out, and the person and their entire family come forward to be presented with the Word of God in their language. I was amazed that they didn't just walk forward to receive it—they shouted, danced, praised, and thanked God. It took at least two hours to hand out all the Bibles. The service started at 11:00 a.m. and ended at 5:00 p.m. There was a message, but the majority of the time was spent worshipping and praising God. The people and the atmosphere overflowed with unspeakable joy. I've never given out Bibles in Indonesia, but what touched me the most there was the orphanage children and teens. They praised God during services with what seemed like never-ending energy and enthusiasm. They could dance and praise for hours, and there too joy abounded. Where praise resounds, joy abounds!

PRAYER

Prayer is simply talking to God. Paul instructs us to "*pray without ceasing*" (1 Thessalonians 5:17, NKJV). We are to be in continuous communication with the Lord. We derive great enjoyment and fulfillment from spending time talking with those we love. This should be even more so with our Heavenly Father as we inquire of Him daily. Wonderful joy is found in our intimacy with the Lord. Our closeness with the Lord grows and produces gladness of heart as we commune with Him in prayer. In the same manner that thankfulness and praise bring us into the presence of the Lord, so does prayer. Dwelling in His presence daily will cause great joy.

My husband was a journeyman plumber and was one of the best plumbers around. He was a perfectionist! He'd put a level on his pipes to make sure they were straight. He was excellent at working with his hands, yet he struggled with reading and writing things down. He had to write a test to obtain his journeyman plumbers ticket. He struggled and failed the first two times, but before he wrote the test for the third time, we prayed that the Lord would help him pass. I remember the Lord saying, "He will pass it this time," so I passed that on to Clarence.

He smiled and said, "Well, I know you can hear from God, so if you say I'm going to pass, I'm going to pass." Great joy began to rise up in me as I thought of how God was about to answer our prayer. A few days later, Clarence wrote the exam. It took a few weeks to get the results. When they arrived, he looked at them and said he'd failed again. I just started laughing out loud and said, "Whose report will you believe? I believe the report of the Lord—you passed!"

Clarence called the apprenticeship board and told them he wanted the test re-marked. They didn't usually do that, but because Clarence said that he knew he'd passed, they agreed. They found a few places where they'd marked an answer wrong when it was right, so he passed. It was all because we prayed, rejoiced, and trusted in the Lord. Prayer is powerful and brings results that cause great joy.

Many times over the years as I've prayed, joy has overwhelmed me. I'm part of a small group of ladies from our church who pray together once a week, and we've had some very powerful prayer times. Often we've been overcome with joy as the Lord has shown us things and answered our prayers. One evening as we were praying, the Lord showed me a picture of a large oil-can with a long spout. He was pouring oil out of it and over each one of us. God spoke to me: "I am anointing you with the oil of gladness as you pour out your hearts to me in prayer." I told the ladies this, and joy overtook us as we began to laugh and thank the Lord for answering our prayers. When you pray in faith, joy in the Holy Ghost will be the end result.

Before Jesus ascended into Heaven, He told His disciples to stay in Jerusalem until they received the Holy Spirit. They left the Mount of Olives and returned to Jerusalem to the upper room, where they'd been lodging. They spent time in continual, unified prayer, making their requests to God. When the Day of Pentecost came, they were all together in the upper room. They heard a noise that sounded like a violent windstorm. The sound engulfed the entire room, and fire that looked like tongues became visible, settling upon each one and filling them with the Holy Spirit.

If we stay in God's presence in a posture of prayer, the Holy Spirit will manifest to us, just as He did on that day. He will fill us and refill us, causing us to rejoice and be glad. As those who had been filled left the upper room, people thought they were drunk. Peter stood up and spoke to them for a long time, explaining what had happened and how God had raised Jesus from the dead. Many believed in the Lord, and they met together daily to pray, take part in communion, and fellowship with each other: "*They spent their time in learning from the apostles, taking part in the fellowship meals and the prayers*" (Acts 2:42, GNT); "*Day after day they met as a group in the temple, and they had their meals together in their homes, eating with glad and humble hearts, praising God, and enjoying the goodwill of all the people*" (Acts 2:46–47a, GNT).

Through prayer we are joined to the vinedresser. It's through that connection to the Father, Son, and Holy Spirit that we receive the spiritual nourishment necessary to grow and produce the fruit of joy, plus all the other fruits of the Spirit. We can't bear fruit unless we pray and spend time with our Heavenly Father, the vinedresser; Jesus, the vine; and the Spirit, the fruit producer. The Passion Translation explains this truth well:

So you must remain in life—union with me, for I remain in life—union with you. For as a branch severed from the vine will not bear fruit, so your life will be fruitless unless you live your life intimately joined to mine.

—John 15:4, TPT

Paul and Silas serve as another great example. When imprisoned and in chains, they prayed and sang to the Lord. Suddenly, around midnight, there was an earthquake, and they and all the prisoners were set free. When we pray, God shows up in a mighty way! I believe that their prayers and singing were loud and joyous, because all the prisoners heard them. The other inmates discovered that when you pray, rejoice, trust God, and stay in a place of joy instead of fear and anxiety, your prayers and praises will produce love, joy, and peace in the Holy Spirit.

As always, Jesus is our best example. He prayed and kept in touch with His Father continually and had a close, intimate relationship with Him. Jesus said that He did nothing on His own, but only what His Father told Him. The disciples observed Jesus as He communicated with His Father, and they wanted what He had. For that reason, one of the disciples asked Jesus to teach them to pray.

Jesus had joy in abundance, and the disciples would have seen how being with His Father caused Him to be very joyful. Jesus wanted His disciples to have that same joy: "*My purpose for telling you these things is so that the joy that I experience will fill your hearts with overflowing gladness*" (John 15:11, TPT). Jesus had the oil of gladness poured on Him more than anyone else, as it says in both Hebrews 1:9 and Psalms 45:7, and He wants us to have that same joy. Abiding in His presence with thanksgiving, prayers, and praise will ensure lasting and overflowing joy in our lives.

KEYS TO JOY—PART TWO
Chapter Six

"I rejoice in your word like one who discover a great treasure."
—Psalms 119:162, NLT

Each of the first three keys enables us to access joy. The remaining keys are also essential for a joy-filled life.

GOD'S WORD

God's Word is at work in believers when we take the time to read, meditate, and instill the scriptures into our hearts and minds. Several years ago, I and three other ladies went to minister at a nursing home a couple of times a month. The Lord had clearly spoken to me about being a part of that outreach. I wasn't in charge and didn't do the preaching; I just went along to visit and pray with the seniors, and I was quite content to do so. I had no desire to preach.

One day the person who usually preached said to me: "I want you to preach." I really didn't want to, but I felt the Lord prompting me to do it. I spent many hours studying and meditating on the Word in preparation. I was very nervous, but the Lord just said, "Declare my Word over yourself." In my personal time with the Lord, I began to speak over myself that, just like Jeremiah and Paul, the Holy Spirit would take over when I opened my mouth. I declared that I could do all things through Christ who strengthened me, and that greater was He who was in me than He who was in the world.

I got up to speak that first time with fear and trembling, but once I began, joy and peace overwhelmed me. I loved it and thought it was actually fun to preach the Word. A few months later, the lady in charge moved away, and the outreach director from my church asked me if I'd take over the preaching. He told me that he'd prayed, and he believed I was the one who was supposed to do this. He said he was confident that I was quite capable.

I preached in that outreach for ten years. This experience gave me confidence in myself (knowing the Holy Spirit was with me) to minister on the street and on the mission field. I still get nervous, which I believe is a good thing because you realize you can't do it in your own strength. Whenever I speak, teach, or get up and give a word of encouragement or share something the Lord has shown me from His Word, joy is always the result.

The Israelites were commanded to keep the commandments and laws given to Moses by God. They were told to impress them into their own minds and hearts and then teach them to their children.

> *And these words which I am commanding you this day shall be [first] in your [own] minds and hearts; [then] You shall whet and sharpen them as to make them penetrate, and teach*

and impress them diligently upon the [minds and] hearts of your children, and shall talk of them when you sit in your house and when you walk by the way, and when you lie down and when you rise up. And you shall bind them as a sign upon your hand, and they shall be as frontlets (forehead bands) between your eyes. And you shall write them upon the doorposts of your house and on your gates.

—Deuteronomy 6:6–9, AMPC

As we continually put the Word of God before us, it will work mightily on our behalf— instructing, encouraging, admonishing, directing, and guiding us. Most wonderfully, it will fill us with great joy as we choose to meditate on, believe, trust in, and rely on its truths.

Sadly, many Christians find it a drudgery to read their Bibles. They think it's boring and uninteresting. Many say it's not relevant for today. How sad! God wants us to enjoy the time we spend reading, studying, and meditating upon His Word. The Merriam Webster dictionary states that to meditate on something means "to focus one's thoughts on, reflect or ponder over."[20] Psalm 1 tells us that a blessed person is one who doesn't follow the advice of the wicked or hang out with them but delights in God's Word, and they meditate on it continually. "*Instead, they find joy in obeying the Law of the Lord, and*

---

20 *Merriam-Webster*, s.v. "meditate," accessed November 18, 2018, https://www.merriam-webster.com/dictionary/meditate.

they study it day and night" (Psalm 1:2, GNT); "*Oh, how I love Your law! It is my meditation all the day*" (Psalm 119:97, NKJV). The phrase "*study it day and night*" tells us that we are to daily keep the scriptures before us, fixing our minds and hearts on them continually. The Word of God will nourish and feed our heart and soul as we take delight in it. The Prophet Jeremiah said, "*Your words were found and I ate them, And Your words became a joy to me and the delight of my heart ...*" (Jeremiah 15:16a, AMP).

When we were born again, we received the nature of God. Our spirits were reborn, and we were given God's Spirit to dwell within us. The Holy Spirit gives us the desire for and ability to understand God's Word. With knowledge and understanding comes joy. Through the Spirit, we're able to conquer the evil desires of the flesh, allowing the Word to take precedence in our lives and fill us with joy. "*For I joyfully concur with the law of God in the inner man*" (Romans 7:22, NASB).

Our intimate relationship with our Father in heaven through the Holy Spirit is invaluable to our understanding of scripture. To experience joy in reading the Bible, we must allow the Holy Spirit to reveal its truths to our hearts. When we gain revelation from the Word of God, we find ourselves rejoicing in those truths! The book of Proverbs explains how a good word gives joy to our heart. A reassuring word will counteract concern, stress, anxiety, fear, and depression, filling us with indescribable joy. "*Anxious fear brings depression, but a life-giving word of encouragement can do wonders to restore joy to the heart*" (Proverbs 12:25, TPT).

Keys to Joy—Part Two

We find joy when we obey the Word. God commands us to delight, or take great satisfaction from, the Word. He insists that we meditate on it daily. We must act upon His Word, not just hear it and ignore it. James admonishes us to be doers of the Word and not just hearers. He says that we'll find joy in the doing:

But whoever catches a glimpse of the revealed counsel of God—the free life!—even out of the corner of his eye, and sticks with it, is no distracted scatterbrain but a man or woman of action. That person will find delight and affirmation in the action.

—James 1:25, MSG

All scripture is inspired by God and entirely true. Walking in the truth of God's Word brings joy. John exclaimed:

I was filled with joy and delight when the brothers arrived and informed me of your faithfulness to the truth. They told me how you live continually in the truth of Christ. It is the greatest joy of my life to hear that my children are consistently living their lives in the ways of truth!

—3 John 1:3–4, TPT

We can completely trust in the Word of God, as every word is full of truth: "*Every promise from the faithful God is pure and proves to be true ...*" (Proverbs 30:5a, TPT).

Pure Joy

Jesus told His disciples that if they adhered to His commandments, they would abide in His love in the same way that He followed His Father's instructions and remained in His love. He explained that His purpose for speaking those words was to incite joy: "*I have told you these things so that you can have the same joy I have and so that your joy will be the fullest possible joy*" (John: 15:11, NCV).

God's Word is a priceless commodity in the lives of believers. When we read, meditate, study, and obey its truths, we rejoice in it as one who has found a precious treasure. "*Your promises are the source of my bubbling joy; the revelation of your word thrills me like one who has discovered hidden treasure*" (Psalm 119:162, TPT).

Serving

We're told in scripture to "*... serve the Lord with gladness ...*" (Psalm 100:2a, NKJV). There's great joy to be found in serving! We must purposely choose to enjoy serving, even if it's as mundane as cleaning the church washroom. We need to have a right heart attitude and do whatever we are asked as unto the Lord. If we're not enjoying serving, we need to stop and take a hard look at our attitude. Paul says to do everything wholeheartedly, as it's Jesus Christ we're serving and not man: "*Do your work willingly, as though you were serving the Lord himself, and not your earthly master. In fact, the Lord Christ is the one you are really serving ...*" (Colossians 3:23–24a, CEV).

I learned early on as a new believer how satisfying and enjoyable it is to serve the body of Christ. Before I became a Christian, I'd taken my early childhood education training and was working in a child care centre. When I got saved, my boyfriend, his sister, and I started attending a small country church that averaged around thirty people a service. As soon as people found out that I worked with children, the pastor's wife asked me to teach Sunday school. I was a bit nervous, as I knew little about the Bible at that point. She told me that it didn't matter, as the lessons were set out in the Sunday school material, so I could just follow it.

I had so much fun teaching those children. I'd get very excited when it was my week to teach. I helped out in other areas too, like cleaning the church. I just enjoyed serving. After getting married and moving away from the area, I went back for several summers and taught Vacation Bible School. I've served in different ways over the years, and I've remained involved in children's ministry for thirty-three years. At times I've felt frustrated, or would rather have been in a service, but if you serve as unto the Lord with gladness, as the Bible teaches, it's always a fun and enjoyable time. Joy always comes when you do what the Lord asks of you, and one of the things he wants us to do is serve.

Serving entails more than just menial tasks, overseeing a department in your church, working in an area such as children's ministry, or even preaching and teaching the Word. It's worship, showing kindness, making a meal, offering to go and pray for someone, or taking an interest in a new person at church by inviting them over for dinner or out for coffee. It's giving yourself entirely to the Lord: your time, gifts, talents, abilities, finances—your whole life.

Serving encompasses thanksgiving, praise, prayer, and spending time in the Word. In the story of Mary and Martha, Mary served by sitting at the feet of Jesus, just as Martha served by fixing dinner for Him. Martha was distracted in doing for Jesus instead of serving Him by giving Him her time. We're being a servant when we read the Word, pray, praise, spend time in church listening to the teaching of the Word, tell others about the Lord, or help one another.

Unfortunately, we have many Marthas in the body of Christ today. They're too busy serving the flesh, working extra hours at their job, and running their children around to different activities. They're distracted by many things yet under the delusion that they're still living for and serving God because they show up at church once in a while. They often come because it's their turn to help out in the nursery, or usher, and they resent never being in a church service.

Sometimes people complain that helping out isn't fun anymore. Martha didn't enjoy what she was doing and saw it as an obligation; otherwise, she never would have complained to Jesus that Mary wasn't helping her. Mary chose wisely to serve her Lord by abiding in His presence: "*The Lord answered her, 'Martha, Martha, you are worried and upset about many things, but one thing is necessary. Mary has made the right choice, and it will not be taken away from her*'" (Luke 10:41, CSB). Mother Teresa once said that "Holy living consists in doing God's work with a smile."[21]

We will only love, honour, and serve God and others with sincerity of heart when we overflow with joyful enthusiasm that comes from the Spirit. Paul wrote: "*Never be lacking in zeal, but keep your spiritual fervor, serving the Lord*" (Romans 12:11).

SHARING/SALVATION

There's nothing more satisfying than sharing Christ with others. Telling others about the love of God and the redemption that comes through Him is exhilarating. Your spirit just leaps with joy, especially when others accept the truth and allow you to lead them in a prayer of salvation. Excitement wells up inside them and you.

The joy we experience at the new birth only increases as we gain understanding of what the Lord did for us on the cross and the eternal future we have to look forward to with Him. Thinking of what lies ahead should spark a desire in us to share the good news with others. We are commanded to go into all the world and preach the gospel. Like with many other commands, it's something we're to do every day: "*Sing to the Lord, bless His name; Proclaim the good news of His salvation from day to day*" (Psalm 96:2, NKJV).

---

[21] "Mother Teresa Quotes," AZ Quotes, accessed November 9, 2018, https://www.azquotes.com/author/14530-Mother_Teresa.

Pure Joy

There are many examples throughout the New Testament of people rejoicing with the joy that comes from accepting Christ's salvation, or from returning to their first love. Jesus tells three parables in Luke 15: the lost sheep, the lost coin, and the prodigal son.

In the first story, Jesus tells of the shepherd leaving the ninety-nine and going after the one that was lost.

> *There once was a shepherd with a hundred lambs, but one of the lambs wandered away and was lost. So the shepherd left the ninety-nine lambs out in the open field and searched the wilderness for the one lost lamb. He didn't stop until he found it. With exuberant joy he raised it up and placed it on his shoulders, carrying it back with cheerful delight!*
> —Luke 15:4–5, TPT

We should never quit going after the lost and always rejoice when they're found. Heaven always rejoices over one sinner who repents, and so should we.

Jesus tells another story about a lost coin. In this parable, a woman has ten silver coins but loses one. She sweeps and cleans her house until she finds the missing coin. She then calls all her friends and neighbours together to rejoice with her, because she found her lost coin.

> *When she finally found it, she gathered all her friends and neighbors for a celebration, telling them "Come and celebrate with me! I had lost my precious silver coin, but now I've found*

it." That's the way God responds every time one lost inner repents and turns to him. He says to all his angels "Let's have a joyous celebration, for that one who was lost I have found!"
—Luke 15:9–10, TPT

There is joy here on earth and in heaven when people repent and receive Jesus as Lord and Saviour. When people come to the Lord, joy is always the result.

In the final parable in this chapter, the prodigal son returns after living an unrighteous life. The father forgives him and rejoices that his son has come home. He throws a big party for his son. When the older son comes home from working in the field, he hears the music and dancing and asks the servant what's going on. When he finds out that his father is having a party in honour of his younger brother, he becomes very angry and refuses to attend. The father comes out and begs the older brother to come celebrate. The older son reminds his father of how he has always done what his father asked of him and remained with him all these years, yet he never held a celebration for him. The father explains that all he has belongs to him, but it's right to be glad and rejoice when someone you thought was dead is alive again, or was lost but is found. We should never be upset when someone rededicates their life to the Lord. If we really love them the way our Heavenly Father does, we will rejoice and be full of joy and celebrate their return. "*It's only right to celebrate like this and be overjoyed, because this brother of yours was once dead and gone, but now he is alive and back with us again. He was lost but now he is found*" (Luke15:32, TPT).

Pure Joy

Jesus told these parables to help the disciples understand the joy the Father experiences, and which we should share, when people come to Christ. The book of Acts records accounts of people being converted and the joy and rejoicing that arose because of it.

Acts 8 contains the story of Philip the evangelist. He goes to Samaria and preaches Christ to the people there. They eagerly receive his message when they see the miracles, signs, and wonders, causing the city to overflow with joy: "*This resulted in an uncontainable joy filling the city!*" (Acts 8:8, TPT). Sharing the good news will always cause joy in both the one ministering and the one receiving.

In Acts 10 we find the story of Paul and Silas, who had been unjustly confined in chains. At midnight they began praying and praising loudly. God then sent an earthquake and freed all the prisoners. The jailer was going to kill himself, because he knew he'd be in big trouble with his superiors. Paul told him not to harm himself, as they were all there. The prison guard brought them out and asked them how he could be saved. Paul and Silas explained the way of salvation to him and his household. "*The jailer and all his family were filled with joy in their newfound faith in God*" (Acts 16:34, TPT).

When my friend Pat and I were on a mission trip to Kenya a few years ago, we participated in what they called hut-to-hut ministry. We took food and household items to different homes and shared Jesus and prayed with the families. We went into one hut where a young couple lived. The husband was drunk, so we talked to him and his wife and asked them if they knew

Jesus. This man used the exact same words as the jailer in Acts: "What must I do to be saved?" We shared the gospel and led them in a salvation prayer. After we finished praying, we realized that he had completely sobered up. He wasn't drunk anymore, and he was rejoicing and praising God. To this day, he has never had another drink, and he and his wife are faithfully serving the Lord. They were filled with joy, and so were we. We could hardly contain our joy and excitement upon witnessing the radical change in them.

In the book of Isaiah, we're told: "*Therefore with joy we will draw water from the wells of salvation*" (Isaiah 12:3, NKJV). John tells the story of Jesus and the Samaritan woman at the well. Jesus asks her for a drink of water. This surprises her, because she's a Samaritan, and the Jews would have nothing to do with them. Jesus tells the woman that if she knew who had asked her for a drink, she would have asked Him for living water. He explains that those who drink from that well will thirst again, but those who drink of the water that comes from Him will never be thirsty.

Jesus answered, "If you drink from Jacob's well you'll be thirsty again and again, but if anyone drinks the living water I give them, they will never thirst again and will be forever satisfied! For when you drink the water I give you it becomes a gushing fountain of the Holy Spirit, springing up and flooding you with endless life!'"

—John 4:13, TPT

The Lord is a well of eternal life and a river of living water. When we drink of Him, joy will flow.

Faith

The last key is faith. The Bible makes it very clear that without faith, it's impossible to please God. When we walk in the Spirit and allow Him to lead us, we walk by faith—and that pleases the Father: "*Now faith is the substance of things hoped for, the evidence of things not seen*" (Hebrews 11:1, NKJV). The Message Bible says it well:

> *The fundamental fact of existence is that this trust in God, this faith, is the firm foundation under everything that makes life worth living. It's our handle on what we can't see. The act of faith is what distinguished our ancestors, set them above the crowd.*
>
> —Hebrews 11:1–2, MSG

Just as faith set our forefathers apart, today it distinguishes the believer in Christ from the unbeliever. Trusting, believing, and having faith are all synonymous. It takes faith to have joy. When we received the Holy Spirit, the fruit of the Spirit was deposited into our recreated spirits in seed form. Initially we might not see much evidence that the fruits exist, but as we grow and mature in our faith, they become increasingly more evident in our lives. We won't ever experience never-ending joy unless we believe it's God's will for us to have it. We must

Keys to Joy—Part Two

have faith and believe in the one who is faithful. If we seem to be running low on joy, we need to check our faith meter. We are called believers because we believe.

We have all heard people say: "I'll believe it when I see it." But that's not faith! Faith says "I believe, so I know I will see." It's speaking what we know is true despite the circumstances. I sang this little song that I made up with my children when they were young, just to emphasize to them the importance of speaking God's Word with faith, believing:

> Speak, speak, speak the Word,
> Speak the Word each day.
> Speak, speak, speak the Word
> The devil runs away!
> Speak, speak, speak the Word,
> Speak the Word each day.
> Speak, speak, speak the Word
> Sickness cannot stay!

I wanted my children to understand that there is power in the Word of God, and that when we believe it and speak it with authority, things happen. "*And since we have the same spirit of faith, according to what is written, 'I believed and therefore I spoke,' we also believe and therefore speak*" (2 Corinthians 4:13, NKJV).

Jesus told His disciples that if they had faith and didn't doubt, they could say to the mountain "Be cast into the sea," and it would be done. He also told them that if they had faith the size of a mustard seed, they could say to the mountain

"Move," and it would move! It doesn't take a lot of faith—a mustard seed is very small. We just need a glimpse of the truth. We're all given a measure of faith. We don't have a lot of faith when we first accept Jesus, but we have enough to believe the truth of God's Word. As we grow and mature in the Lord, our faith grows.

God told Abraham to look and see, that the Lord was giving him all the land he saw. Jesus told the ruler of the synagogue to only believe, and his daughter would be made well. The woman with an issue of blood spoke, acted, and believed that when she touched the hem of Jesus' garment, she would be made whole. Jesus told her that it was her faith that made her whole.

Paul in his writings to the churches makes the connection between trust and joy:

> *May the God of hope fill you with all joy and peace in believing [through the experience of your faith] that by the power of the Holy Spirit you will abound in hope and overflow with confidence in His promises.*
>
> —Romans 15:13, AMP

When we believe, we will be full of joy. Paul also writes that if we declare with our mouth and believe with our heart that God raised Christ from the dead, we will be saved (Romans 10:9–10).

Peter connects believing with the joy of salvation:

Keys to Joy—Part Two

Without having seen Him, you love Him; though you do not [even] now see Him, you believe in Him and exult and thrill with inexpressible and glorious (triumphant, heavenly) joy. [At the same time] you receive the result (outcome, consummation) of your faith, the salvation of your souls.

—1 Peter 1:8–9, AMPC

The psalmist often unites trust and believing with joy, rejoicing, and gladness: "*For our heart is glad in him, because we trust in his holy name*" (Psalm 33:21, ESV).

Joy comes when we believe and have faith in God's Word, particularly the words of Christ, and act on them. John records Jesus's words about the importance of believing and asking, so that our joy will be full.

So will you also pass through a time of intense sorrow when I am taken from you, but you will see me again! And then your hearts will burst with joy, with no one being able to take it from you! For here is eternal truth: When that time comes you won't need to ask me anything, but instead you will go directly to the Father and ask him for anything you desire and he will give it to you, because of your relationship with me. Until now you've not been bold enough to ask the Father for a single thing in my name, but now you can ask, and keep on asking him! And you can be sure that you'll receive what you ask for, and your joy will have no limits!

—John 16:22–24, TPT

Pure Joy

We can boldly come to the throne of grace in time of need and ask anything in Jesus' name, and He will do it for us. That is faith in action, and the result will be fullness of joy.

We can have faith in the most difficult of situations. No one likes to go through hardships and troubles, or to feel sorrow and grief, or physical or emotion pain, but no troublesome circumstance will last forever. If we believe, joy will come: "... *We may weep through the night, but at daybreak it will turn into shouts of ecstatic joy*" (Psalm 30:5b, TPT). James said:

> *My fellow believers, when it seems as though you are facing nothing but difficulties, see it as an invaluable opportunity to experience the greatest joy that you can! For you know that when your faith is tested it stirs up power within you to endure all things.*
>
> —James 1:2–3, TPT

Paul lived a life of faith. He endured many things, but he never wavered in his belief and trust in the Lord. At the time of his conversion on the road to Damascus, he received an instant revelation of who Jesus was. From that moment on, he lived a faith-filled life. Jesus was always in the forefront of His mind, and he had great love for His Lord and Saviour. He shared his testimony many times, as he was persuaded that the message of the gospel was true and for everyone. Paul believed that nothing could separate us from the love of Christ. He lived by faith through many trials and persecutions with much rejoicing and gladness of heart.

Keys to Joy—Part Two

Jesus endured the cross because of the joy He saw ahead of him. By faith He saw millions upon millions of people who would be born into the Kingdom of God because of His obedience. Nothing will be impossible if we have faith. We'll be rewarded with great joy if we seek the Lord with all our heats:

And without faith living within us it would be impossible to please God. For we come to God in faith knowing that he is real and that he rewards the faith of those who give all their passion and strength into seeking him.

—Hebrews 11:6, TPT

At two years of age, my niece was involved in a freak accident. Her mom was cleaning up around some family gravestones in the cemetery in a small town in Saskatchewan. While she worked, her daughter ran near a gravestone made of marble, and it fell on her. She was rushed to a hospital in the nearby town. The doctors determined that she had a broken jaw and foot, many scrapes and bruises, and internal bleeding. They quickly decided that she should be moved to either Saskatoon or Regina.

"Where do you want us to send her, Saskatoon or Regina?" the doctor asked.

Her mom, not a Christian at the time, said, "Send her to Saskatoon, because my brother and sister-in-law live there. They're Christians and will pray for her."

Michelle called us and told us the details of what had happened and that our niece, Arianna, was on the way by ambulance to Royal University Hospital. We began to pray and intercede for her, and we went to the hospital to meet Clarence's sister when she arrived. We began to rejoice in faith, believing that Arianna was healed.

Upon their arrival, Michelle told us the many negative things the medical staff had said about her daughter's injuries. Laughter rose up in us and we said to Michelle: "Whose report will you believe? We believe the report of the Lord, and Arianna is healed. Every report you get from now on will be good."

Sure enough, the first report came back after the CAT scan and showed that there had been internal bleeding, but it had completely stopped. We encouraged Michelle to rejoice, because God had healed her daughter. Every time the medical staff reported something negative, we told her to rejoice and believe that Arianna was healed. The doctors were stunned. The X-rays taken at the previous hospital showed a broken jaw and foot, but the new X-rays showed that nothing was broken. Joy bubbled up as we put our faith in God.

Faith always rejoices and results in abundant, overflowing joy! All these keys are interconnected, and faith undergirds them all. It takes faith to activate them in our day-to-day life. A lifestyle of living by faith will cause joy to overtake our lives. Faith will cause the joy within to rise up and grow and increase.

CONCLUSION

Joy is an integral, distinguishing mark of a believer's life. It's a fruit of the Spirit, and the Bible tells us that we are known by our fruit. We should be full of joy! Believers in Christ should be the happiest people on the planet. The psalmist sums it all up: "... *Joyful indeed are those whose God is the Lord*" (Psalm 144:15b, NLT).

God's people should have a reputation for being loving, joyful, peaceful, kind-hearted, patient, gentle in spirit, virtuous, faithful and trusting, and in control of our physical desires and emotions. Our joy comes from only one place—the Lord our God. When we spend time daily in God's presence, fellowshipping with the Holy Spirit, we position ourselves to be led and controlled by Him. When we choose to live a life of walking in the Spirit daily, yielding to Him, we won't long for the desires of the flesh but for the fruit that is produced through our relationship with the Holy Spirit: "... *divine love in all its varied expressions: joy that overflows, peace that subdues, patience that endures, kindness in action, a life of virtue, faith that prevails, gentleness of heart, and strength of spirit*" (Galatians 5:22b, TPT).

As believers in Christ, we should desire to operate in and share the fruit of joy with everyone! To be able to successfully accomplish this in our lives, we must understand how to live a pure, continually joyous life, choosing to not allow any hindrances or troubles to rob us of it. Then we will see joy come to fruition in our lives.

Also by the Author

Devotions of the Heart, Book One is the first book in a two-book series. It contains six months' worth of devotionals, written from the acquired wisdom, knowledge, and understanding of scripture that Lorna has obtained through times of prayer, praise, and study of God's Word. Each devotional touches on a wide range of topics that are sure to uplift your soul and inspire you to develop a closer relationship with the Lord as you read and meditate.

Topics include:

- Prayer
- Praise
- God's Presence
- Leading by the Spirit
- Freedom in Christ
- Hope
- Overcoming fear, sorrow, and grief

Be encouraged and uplifted as *Devotions of the Heart* helps you develop even greater intimacy with the Lord.

Devotions of the Heart, Book Two also contains six months' worth of devotionals, combining with *Book One* to provide readers with a full year of guided time with the Lord. The book is filled with biblical truths, written to comfort and exhort the reader.

Topics include:

- The fruit of the Spirit
- Thanksgiving
- Forgiveness
- The person of the Holy Spirit
- Unity
- The mind of Christ
- The armour of God
- The fire of God

Discover a new-found excitement for the Word as you meditate on these devotionals and pursue an even stronger and more intimate relationship with the Lord